DEDICATION

This book is lovingly dedicated to my parents.
To me, they are the epitome of what God intended
a mother and father to be.
It is also dedicated to my son –
my nearest, dearest friend…I love you forever.

When Thou Art Converted

5.21.2010
Susie,
May God bless and
smile upon you and
keep you with perfect
peace. Praying this gift
from Nikki Underwood
will be a blessing to
your life. God bless you,
Dr Roscoe

When
Thou Art
CONVERTED

Dr. Bertha L. Roscoe

WHEN THOU ART CONVERTED

Cover Design by Atinad Designs

© Copyright 2009

SAINT PAUL PRESS, DALLAS, TEXAS

First Printing, 2009

The name SAINT PAUL PRESS and its logo are registered as a trademark in the U.S. patent office.

ISBN-13: 978-0-9825303-3-7

Printed in the U.S.A.

CONTENTS

ACKNOWLEDGMENTS

All thanks to God for the strength, wisdom, and ability to write this book. We acknowledge Chrisella Collins and Jo Zelma Brown who spoke confirmation and completion into my spirit. We also would like to thank my sister, Anna Marie Davis, who allowed use of her poetry and Pastor Rodney Patterson for prayerfully covering this project. We extend sincere gratitude to all who encouraged and supported this endeavor—and to every reader of this book, God bless you. And to my dear son, Shahbu, thanks for all the experiences learned in our life together.

Not Good Enough

If you tried
often enough only
to be beaten down

You learn
to try covertly
or not at all

We learn to live
in reserve; only giving
bits and pieces when
it feels safe

But now, wanting to respond
to a higher calling,
I watch as He destroys
all barriers

Shyness, shame,
guilt, superfluity
are all mowed down
as He takes control

—Anna Marie Davis

INTRODUCTION

To be "in Christ" is a simple admonition of the Bible. If one is a babe, growing in grace and knowledge or a more mature saint, the need for conversion is ever present. Be willing to ask yourself and patiently wait for His response, "have I been truly conformed to the image of Christ." Don't grade your own paper; so to speak, but seriously consider how your life stands in the light of God's Word. Are you willing to consider the possibility of a dark, sinful side that shuns this light? Is there evidence, according to Scripture, that the old man has been removed and the new man in Christ Jesus has been put on? This book provides a simple approach to challenge Christians to deal with where they really are in Christ...not where they think they are. This book will motivate, encourage, and inspire you to examine yourself and see whether or not you have truly been converted.

–Dr. Bertha L. Roscoe
Round Rock, TX

CHAPTER ONE

THE TRUTH OF THE MATTER

As THE WORDS OF THE WOMEN who first reported the resurrection of Jesus seemed to His followers to be as idle tales and they believed them not, so shall this book be to many. But the truth of the matter is, we live our lives as a tale that is told, and as the Psalmist declared, we need the help of the Lord to number our days that we may apply our hearts unto wisdom (Psalm 90:12); not the sensual, devilish wisdom of this present world but the wisdom that is first pure, then peaceable, gentle, and easy to be entreated, full of mercy and good fruits, without partiality, and without hypocrisy (James 3:17). This is the wisdom from above, which is sadly lacking in the lives of many Christians.

Yes, many Christ-like believers display more ungodly characteristics than some non-believers. The fruit of God's Spirit is barely visible in their daily life yet the claim is made that I am saved, sanctified, and full of God's Spirit. How can this be? The truth, perhaps a bitter pill to swallow, remains steadfast and undaunted: many baptized believers are truly saved and sanctified but have never been converted.

If we are to be perfectly honest, many believers, though they have given the preacher their hand, have never given God their heart. The transformation from worldliness to Godliness has not occurred and thus, they are incapable of living a Spirit-filled life consistently. How can one live "Spirit-filled" when they have only been "Spirit-touched"?

The quickening, emotional charge that many souls have yielded to was the fluttering life, seeking release and nourishment to grow within the believer's heart. As an embryo seeks food from the womb of its mother, so the quickened Spirit seeks spiritual food to grow thereby. Time and time again this quickening has been perceived as the filling of the Spirit and has quenched many a hungering soul with the misconception that *this* is it. This "fluttering" is only proof that there is life within, "...*Christ in you, the hope of glory*" (Colossians 3:27).

But this fluttering is only the beginning of another stage in the cycle of life. In the natural process of formation, once the embryo forms basic bodily shapes and organs, it becomes a fetus. It is still within the womb and must be birthed for independent life to begin. Once the delivery has occurred, immediately the nose and mouth must be cleared of fluid so the baby can commence to breath. At this time, the umbilical cord is cut and tied and the third and final stage of delivery occurs–the afterbirth.

The afterbirth occurs when life-giving mechanisms from within are expelled from the body and the bleeding is stopped. No longer are the mother and child connected by any physical means; their only means of connection must now begin to develop through bonding–the formation of a close and special relationship.

Many a soul is still within the womb of the Spirit; the embryo has yet to develop into a fetus–the heart and mind is undeveloped and yet this soul clamors for the deliverance to occur. But God, in His infinite wisdom and love does not bring forth abnormal or dysfunctional children. He allows no embryo to come forth from the womb nor allows premature birthing to occur. Even Paul, in his letter to the Galatians states, *"my little children, of whom I travail in birth again until Christ be formed in you"* (Galatians 4:19).

"Shall I bring to the birth, and not cause to bring forth? saith the Lord: shall I bring forth, and shut the womb? saith thy God" (Isaiah 66:9).

Other souls have been brought forth, yet the clearing of the nose and mouth was not endured and thus, they have not been infused with the *pneuma,* or breath of life. They have existence outside the womb but you cannot live without breathing.

This soul, because of its inability to breathe holds on to the cord for life and does not allow the afterbirth to occur. There is constant repentance of dead works and continuous bleeding. Christ is being crucified afresh by the soul in this state and the bonding process cannot begin–but if this soul yields itself to God, it can go on unto perfection (maturity).

This is the relevance of the conversation between Christ and Nicodemus, whose name means *victorious over the people*. Christ told him, *"...except a man be born again, he cannot see the kingdom of God."* But the dialogue continues, and Christ further states, *"...except a man be born of water and of the Spirit, he cannot enter into the kingdom of God."* There are some who will only get to "see" the kingdom without being allowed to enter. Therefore, it behooves us to confront the truth of the matter and realize the condition we are really in that we might be set free and go on unto perfection.

If we do not become victorious over what people may think or say about us and allow such fear to keep us in the stages of development so that we never form a close, special relationship with God through His Son, then we are destined to only see His kingdom. Christ told His disciples in Matthew 10:28, *"...fear not them which kill the body, but are not able to kill the soul: but rather fear Him which is able to destroy both soul and body in hell."*

To say such a thing as this in the midst of a believing congregation would enrage many a saint; ears would be closed, hearts would be hardened, and indignation would rise. But one honest soul, longing and thirsting for a deeper, more meaningful relationship with God, would open their heart and humbly declare as the Canaanite woman who relentlessly sought a blessing from the Lord, *"Truth, Lord"* (Matthew 15:22-28). This honest soul would secretly admit, "I am saved, but have never been converted."

But the shame, humiliation, and even sorrow would hinder that soul from making a public declaration. How can I say such a thing? Simply because I was once that honest soul that sat in dumbfounded sorrow, ashamed to admit such a thing had not only been revealed to me, but also that I had been found guilty. I was saved, and truly believed that I was sanctified and Holy Ghost filled, yet the Lord spoke to my heart that I had not yet been converted.

Time and time again, I've sat in church services witnessing an extreme contrast between what was said and what was done, even seeing so many schisms within the body. How we must grieve the Spirit of the Lord as we take time for so many things on "our program" but when it comes time for the spoken Word to be preached or taught, we paraphrase or skip its reading *in the interest of time*. It's no wonder that God has a controversy with us (Hosea 4:1).

We think we are when we are not; so we often do as Peter and make bold declarations yet lack the strength and spiritual stamina to fulfill those statements. We grow weary in well doing and often find the zeal of living holy absent in our day-to-day life. The Lord stirred this writing within to challenge the believer who knows this to be true, to have faith in Him and to admit that I am unable to strengthen my brother and/or my sister because I have not been converted.

Now the enemy would have the saint to feel ashamed of such a statement and to reflect the heavenly mirror upon another in denial of the fact that it's me, oh, Lord, in need of conversion. To embrace the truth of God's Word and release lying vanity is the only way to receive the mercy of God and receive conversion of the soul.

Hope maketh not ashamed and we are justified by faith in God. Rather than pointing the finger as Adam did to Eve, and Eve did to the serpent that beguiled her, we must honestly take responsibility for our own soul and hold fast to the love of God and seek all that He has for us on this side of glory.

I do not want to live a mediocre life, unfulfilled, and denied of all that God has for me. A full release is what my soul longs for so I must face the darkness within, earnestly seek God's deliverance, and go on unto perfection. Jesus states, *"Verily I say unto you, except ye be converted, and become as little children, ye shall not enter into the kingdom of heaven"* (Matthew 18:3). Once true conversion occurs, then we can strengthen others.

An analogy impressed upon my heart by the Spirit of God was to imagine yourself walking down a long hallway. You come to a room and upon opening the door, you allow the light to be turned on. As you look around the room, you see utter chaos and total disarray of the things within.

This is the heart of many saints. To shut the door as though you have no knowledge of such a room or in hopes of it "magically" being put aright is a refusal to allow the Lord to examine your inner being. You can become bothered and disillusioned by the disorder and yet close the door encasing it in the former darkness and proceed on down the hall. But the knowledge of "that" room will haunt you.

Closing the door does not eliminate the need for that particular room to be purified. The Lord does not ask nor expect us to clean the chambers of our heart; He simply wants us to submit ourselves to Him. He does the work.

Far too many lose heart because of the great task they think is involved in cleaning this room. They attempt to take it upon themselves and become overwhelmed with the work to be done. God only wants us to leave the light on and admit that the room is in need of cleaning. The response, when conviction occurs, is simply, "Yes, Lord, I will proceed no further until this room is put in order." To go on in spite of and in the midst of the chaos is detrimental to one's spiritual growth.

CHAPTER TWO

CONVICTION IS NOT CONVERSION

THE HOLY SPIRIT HAS CONVICTED many souls of sin. This conviction is only the first stage in the process of repentance and leads to acknowledgment and confession. Far too long have we mishandled and misunderstood this process and allowed a short cut viewing of this initial step as the conclusion of the whole matter.

When David sinned before God having slept with Bathsheba and having her husband purposely slain in battle, he was about to settle into his sinful state. He had committed adultery and murder and covered up his acts. He was nowhere near acknowledgment, confession, nor repentance. He had a new wife and a son on the way, but God's hand was heavy upon him.

Deceit was added to his list of sinful acts because in hiding his wrongdoing, he despised the commandment of the Lord. This man after God's own heart, had displeased the Lord by his secret actions. But the thing was not hid from God. He sent Nathan, the prophet, to the king of Israel and exposed the whole situation, because by his actions, the leader of the nation had "...*given great occasion to the enemies of the Lord*."

David was accurately accused by Nathan and had heard the pronouncement of God's judgment prior to his acknowledgment and confession stating, *"I have sinned against the Lord."* This statement was not repentance, but the sincerity and the grief over having displeased God. David found out that though no one knew of his actions, the matter was not hid from God.

Exposure to the truth brought him to the point of conviction, which led to acknowledgment and confession of sin against God, and mercifully, to true repentance (see Psalm 51). After this, David was forgiven by God and restored to fellowship but he yet had to bear the consequences for his sinful actions (II Samuel 11:27; 12:1-20).

Only exposure to the truth can lead to conviction of sin. Conviction is the realization of wrongdoing against God and is accompanied by overwhelming sorrow, which causes one to cry out to God for forgiveness and cleansing. The focus is not centralized on the sinful act but rather the displeasure of God because of a sinful nature.

This sinful nature causes one to commit acts that separate him from the presence of God and thus the heart cries out because only in His presence is there fullness of joy (Psalm 16:11). So to be separated from His presence is to lose one's joy. We can do as David, and attempt to settle to a life of secret sin, but sooner or later, the displeasure of God will become unbearable.

Now when this occurs, we cannot pamper the torn soul with placable reassurances. This wrenching of the soul is a necessary part of the process. This, my friend, is heart-felt conviction for sinning against God.

When Achan sinned and brought an accursed thing into the camp of the Israelites, even though he buried the accursed thing under his tent, God saw it and was not pleased. Joshua, the leader of the Israelites at that time, admonished Achan to, *"give, I pray thee, glory to the Lord God of Israel, and make confession unto Him; and tell me now what thou hast done; hide it not from me."*

Achan's honest response to the conviction brought glory to God. He answered Joshua, *"I have sinned against the Lord God of Israel, and thus and thus have I done"* (Joshua 7). Conviction led to acknowledgment and acknowledgment led to confession. Conviction is acceptance of the truth and the realization of being opposed to what is right.

It is neither acknowledgment nor confession, thus it is not repentance, it is conviction. We have often mistaken this as repentance and established our own righteousness and have not submitted unto the righteousness of God. And thus, the convicted soul has been rushed through the process of repentance without receiving true conversion.

Even though the prodigal son returned home to a joyous father, all ready to forgive and forget, he realized his sin and acknowledged and confessed his error against Heaven and his father. When he came to himself while feeding the swine (exposure to the truth), he recalled the wealth of his father and said to himself, *"I will arise and go to my father, and will say unto him, Father, I have sinned against heaven, and before thee"* (Luke 15:18). Though the father lavished him with love, it was still necessary for this declaration to be made by the son.

I have witnessed many prodigals returning home (and was one of the number) that were "let off the hook." The tears of conviction were all that was required of the church, and I was restored, but God was not pleased. David stated in Psalm 51:3-4, *"...I acknowledge my transgressions: and my sin is ever before me. Against thee, thee only, have I sinned and done this evil in thy sight...."*

He had done wrong to Bathsheba and her husband, Uriah, and even to the nation of Israel as their king, yet he states to God, *"...against thee only have I sinned."* Generally speaking, we are too quick and ready to acknowledge and confess our deeds to one another without first yielding to the conviction of God.

Acknowledgment and confession is more than just an act; it is coming to terms with the fact that one has sinned against God. It is to be brought face-to-face with my true state of sinfulness and separation from God and humbly long for His compassion, forgiveness, and restoration. This is true repentance. I cannot boast of what I did, nor take it for granted that God will forgive, for He is looking at the heart and knows my thoughts and intents.

Am I seeking solace for my wandering soul yet in the far country of sinfulness, or only wanting to grab a quick snack from the saint's feast of charity, or obtain only a quick touch from God without touching Him or feeling His embrace? Yes, I can conjure up tears from my duct glands because I was caught in the very act, or perhaps I am in a jam and my back is against the wall. This is acknowledgment and confession without conviction.

This is temporal and the prodigal soul will soon weary of the way of holiness and venture again into a far country to pursue the pleasures of sin. Disillusioned and beguiled, they will waste the quick snack and the quick touch, settling to live in secret sin as David, had not the prophet exposed his sinful deeds. Sad to say, many Christians are living this very life within the four walls of their church.

This soul will boldly declare, just as Peter did in Luke 22:33, *"Lord I am ready to go with thee, both into prison, and to death,"* only to deny Him a little while later by their sinful deeds. Only when conviction comes through exposure of the truth, acknowledgment and confession is stated (by the wandering soul), and true repentance is forthcoming, can the soul be converted.

Many Christians come to worship services, attend Bible studies, sing in the choir, give their tithes and offerings, and after each service, journey back into a far country to waste their substance in riotous living. This wandering soul will constantly seek prayer, counsel and encouragement, run from one revival to another, attend every seminar and convention and yet have no rest for their soul.

They will do as Judas, who after betraying Christ, repented within himself because he was plagued with guilt. He went back to the chief priests and elders saying, *"I have sinned in that I have betrayed innocent blood,"* and they in turn will say, *"what is that to us? See thou to that"* (Matthew 27:3-4). This wandering soul is willing to go to the church, to preachers, and everyone else sorrowful. But until one goes to God realizing and admitting that it is against Him and Him only that I have sinned, can conviction lead to repentance and forgiveness. Judas, in despair, not finding release from the guilt of shame, hung himself. He did not turn to God nor attempt to go to Christ.

Conviction is brought about because one is convinced of his sinful state and believes that only God can forgive, restore and empower to live an effective Christian life.

The unconverted soul will be known by the fruit that it bears in its self-effort to walk in the Spirit. It will be a tree with beautiful, luscious leaves, and if any, very little fruit.

CHAPTER THREE

WEAK NOT WICKED

WHEN PETER DENIED HIS AFFILIATION with Christ three times, it was not because he did not love his Master. The fact that he wept bitterly upon remembrance of the Lord's prophecy to the very matter implies his repentant spirit and hurt for displeasing God. Of himself, he thought he was ready to go to prison and to death with the Lord but he lacked the spiritual strength to back up the proclamation.

When Jesus foretold Peter of his denial, Jesus knew why, but the matter was hid from Peter until the day of Pentecost when the Holy Ghost was poured out upon them. Until Peter was converted, he relied upon his own strength and knowledge to get by. Even when he declared that Jesus was the Christ, the Lord had to let him know that flesh and blood did not reveal this to him (Matthew 16:16-17).

Peter and the other disciples had been called and chosen by Jesus, but they were not converted until the day of Pentecost. They often misunderstood the teachings of Christ and wearied themselves with petty bickering regarding their understanding of what Jesus' kingdom would be and who would be the greatest in the midst of it.

They rebuked followers seeking a miracle from the Lord, wanting to send them away and doubted the ability of the Lord to feed multitudes of people. They slept in the garden of Gethsemane rather than praying with the Lord and fled in the face of danger—all this, not because they were wicked, but because they were spiritually weak.

Many believers today are doing comparable things not because they are wicked but because they too, are spiritually weak. Paul warned us in his letter to the Romans that in the flesh dwelleth no good thing, *"for to will is present with me; but how to perform that which is good I find not"* (Romans 7:18). The desire to please God is there, but without conversion, one is unable to accomplish all the good intentions of their heart. Consider this portion of David's penitence: *"Create in me a clean heart O God; and renew a right spirit within me. Cast me not away from Thy presence; and take not Thy Holy Spirit from me. Restore unto me the joy of Thy salvation; and uphold me with Thy free spirit. Then will I teach transgressors Thy ways; and sinners shall be converted unto Thee"* (Psalm 51:10-13).

David was not wicked; he was weak. He knew he had disobeyed God and broken His commandments, and we could only speculate on why he sought to cover up his deeds rather than confess them prior to being exposed by the prophet. We cannot even say whether he would have confessed his sin had not the Lord sent Nathan, but we do know the Bible states, *"He that covereth his sins shall not prosper: but whoso confesseth and forsaketh them shall have mercy"* (Proverbs 28:13).

If David had denied his sin or laid the blame on Bathsheba, he would have forsaken the mercy and forgiveness of God. Acknowledgment of sin is not always an easy confession to make. **However, the desire to please God must be greater than the shame of being exposed.** God already knows what we have done. The confession is not to inform Him of our erroneous ways but rather one of the many gracious ways that God exposes our need of Him in order for us to live a holy life.

Refusal to acknowledge and confess is to further displease God. One can be brought to the point of conviction by exposure to the truth and yet despise God by refusing to seek restoration His way. David's weakness did not begin when he slept with Bathsheba; it was only manifested at this time. The weakness began when he did not lead his army into battle. Second Samuel 11:1 states that it *"was at the time when kings go forth to battle"* that David stayed behind in Jerusalem. Because he stayed behind, he saw Bathsheba, and subsequently committed adultery and murder.

Too often, we realize the weakness being manifested, but wait until the deed has caused us separation from God. We rant and rave over the results of the decisions made in our weakened state and seek deliverance without acknowledgment and confession of the root that allowed the stem to grow.

We can, no more than could David, dodge conviction under the claim that I'm only human and was merely caught up in a moment of weakness. This excuse is at best plausible as an attempt to slide into the process of repentance without Godly sorrow or sincerity, and is exposed when we become bitter or rebellious toward the punishment given by God.

When Nathan exposed David's sin, he not only admitted it as true, but he also turned his heart back to God and humbly accepted the Lord's rebuke. David sought God, fasted and prayed, even laid out all night before God, and though forgiven, he had to bear the indignation of the Lord and endure the execution of His judgment.

To balk and scream as though grave injustice is being done against us when we have sinned, denotes the fact that we have not experienced true repentance, nor taken full responsibility and thus we are not in a position to bear the consequences of our actions. When David humbly submitted to the truth of his actions, he received grace to endure the punishment that was measured out to him.

Too often we frustrate the grace of God by continuing in the spiral downfall of a weakened state by not handling things God's way. And thus we will consider fear of letting go as strength for holding on. How often have we witnessed a convicted soul struggling to hold on to a situation that God has clearly spoken for them to release? We see this child of God, quite frankly, having a tantrum and we mistake the tears and the antics as repentance and conversion. And because we allow the "short-cut" to occur and do not properly discern the spirit at work, the convicted soul ventures no further and is not held accountable to acknowledge and confess the truth of the matter.

So as the Lord ministered to the sister, by way of example, to let go of the man that was not her husband, we witnessed her tears of fear and frustration…we saw the expression as she sought God about how this man supported her, her children, and how could she ever make it without him. God never lowers His standard of holiness and was unmoved by her fears knowing that the yielding of her will would release the faith to embrace His grace.

As this soul fought to hold on to her means of support, God sat by and watched. *"Therefore will the Lord wait, that He may be gracious unto you, and therefore will He be exalted, that He may have mercy upon you…"* (Isaiah 30:18). God will wait until we surrender all to follow Him for *"in returning and rest shall we be saved; in quietness and in confidence shall we find strength"* (30:15). But so often, like the children of Israel, we will not trust God enough to let go.

So we do as Saul did when the kingdom was rent from him because of disobedience (I Samuel 15) and seek the approval of man knowing we are not in right standing with God. Saul was told that because he had rejected God's Word, the kingdom of Israel was being taken away from him to be given to one that was better (obedient to God.) Saul's acknowledgment and confession were without conviction, *"I have sinned, yet honor me now…before the elders of my people and before Israel,"* and though his error was covered from the people, God knew and was not pleased.

He admitted his wrong to Samuel but never sought right standing with God. Since his error was not exposed to the public and he had the man of God by his side, he felt justified and continued in disobedience going through the motions as though he truly worshipped God. The rebellious act of Saul had not been corrected. It was not until after ceremonial worship was completed that Samuel (not Saul), carried out the instructions from the Lord and destroyed the enemy. From that point on, the man of God (Samuel) came no more to see Saul until the day of his death (I Samuel 15:30-35).

So I can hold on to the things that God has given me instruction to let go of and continue in the act of worship, in the midst of the saints and the congregation, but is God accepting my sacrifice of praise? Am I being allowed access into His presence or am I being rejected as Saul, yet finding contentment in not being publicly exposed?

This is the true state of many Christians. They are living a life full of secret sin. In their heart, they know the gap is widening between them and God, but the humiliation of public exposure is more than they think they can bear. So they seek to worship in places that will allow them to be comfortable in their current state, and when the Lord graciously exposes their true condition, they draw even further away from His presence, and as David, when he tarried in Jerusalem rather than going into battle with his army, will become lax in the presence of God and begin to have self-confidence and give in to self-indulgence.

Because he had one year of rest from his enemies and a time of peace, David let down his guard and this led to his weakness. Or perhaps he felt a year of rest was not sufficient to restore his strength and did not have the spiritual stamina to return to battle at that time. Whatever his reason, he made a decision without seeking to know the will of God for that matter. And when we take counsel that is not of the Lord, we add sin to sin (Isaiah 30:1).

The Bible states in Ecclesiastes 9:8, *"Let thy garments be always white; and let thy head lack no ointment."* The *let* denotes a choice on my part. Will I allow my garments to remain white and my head to keep oil? The only way this is possible is to remain in the presence of God and to continuously seek His will in every area of my life. The enemy is constantly flinging mud on my garment and trying to rub the oil off my head.

Spiritual weakness on my part opens the door to the enemy. Peter, James, and John slept in the Garden of Gethsemane. They were too weary to pray–so Peter's bold proclamation to go to prison and die with the Lord was just as rash and infeasible as his statement on the Mount of Transfiguration to make three tabernacles (Mark 9:2-10).

Nothing is wrong with the desire other than the fact that it is based on human effort. What requires spiritual fortitude and power injected by and through the Holy Ghost is being attempted with mortal effort and is not sufficient to produce the desired effect. And until conversion occurs, one will see through natural rather than spiritual eyes; one will hear with natural rather than spiritual ears; and one shall perceive but not understand the things of God. Saved, yes, but not yet converted.

This is why the multitude thought Jesus was referring to cannibalism when He told them to eat of His flesh and drink His blood (John 6:51-58). Because they did not understand, they did not believe. This natural way of looking at things is the old sinful nature that must be humbled and brought to the point of conviction for conversion to occur.

CHAPTER FOUR

The Flesh is the Old Nature

THE FLESH ACTS INDEPENDENT OF GOD and places its desires above the will of God. It adds to what God has spoken. Consider Eve's conversation with the serpent in the Garden of Eden (Genesis 3:1-8): the serpent quoted God's command, Eve added to it. When she considered the words of the serpent above the commandment of God, she saw that the tree was good for food and that it was pleasant to the eyes. Flesh seeks to be gratified and satisfied—even if it leads to unholy acts.

We feed the flesh when we fail to get an understanding of God's Word and thus consider things contrary to His holy will. The serpent took advantage of Eve's lack of understanding and seized the opportunity to influence her to act independently of what had been commanded.

Our natural, physical body is not the old nature or the flesh. The flesh is the unregenerate mind, the unborn spirit that cannot comprehend the things of God. This old nature is not good and it is in "this" flesh that no good thing dwelleth. This is the nature that is condemned to death. But if we submit to the will and the ways of God, we die to this nature and we can be born again and be renewed in Christ.

We often mistake our body with its limbs and many members as the flesh, but this is an error. We must feed our natural body in order to survive but we are under no obligation to feed the flesh. The brain ceases to function and dies but the mind lives forever…our mind is the flesh. It is in our mind that we choose whether to obey or disobey God.

In response, either the renewed mind of Christ or the unregenerate carnal mind will dictate our actions. And given such authority, the flesh will work to keep the focus off God because it knows that if the soul is born again of the Spirit, it will have to die. So the claim is made that one belongs to God but yet lives unto themselves and *"they that are after the flesh do mind the things of the flesh"* (Romans 8:5). The flesh becomes its own god.

Such time will be taken to decorate the temple of the fleshly god. It will be lavishly arrayed with intricate artwork, delicately done – oh, how beautifully it is adorned. Great care has been taken in its elegance and grandeur. The flesh demands that its appearance be meticulous for it works in deception and camouflage. The light (lamp) within is polished but there is no oil within to keep it trimmed and burning for David declared, *"Thy Word is a lamp unto my feet and a light unto my path"* (Psalm 119:105).

As in the time of Eli (I Samuel 3:1-3), the flame is all but out, yet we continue to polish the lamp heaping more things to beautify and sustain the grandeur while not rekindling the fire. Thus our praise, our very worship becomes stale and distasteful to God. We attempt to reach Him with a mind that has not been renewed.

The lamp (golden candlestick) within the tabernacle was to be kept burning always. The Lord gave specific instruction that pure oil be used to cause the lamp to burn so that the flame would not go out. (see Exodus 25:31-37; 27:29-21). To use any other oil than that specified by God was to offer "strange fire" and the aroma that exuded was not acceptable. This, my friend, is what the old nature is like.

When we allow our minds to be constantly renewed by the Spirit of God so that we can have the mind of Christ, we are using pure oil to keep our lamp burning always. The fire burns away dross, unholy desires, unholy acts, and deceitfulness. This fire keeps the flesh in subjection and mortifies its deeds.

The body carries out the desires of the nature at work within. If the old nature (mind) desires to commit fornication, the body carries out the deed. If the old nature desires to backbite and gossip, the mouth corresponds and speaks. What is in the spiritual heart and mind is the old nature and is the flesh that must be crucified with Christ or it will remain at work.

The flesh serves the law because it is a law unto itself and thus will bring forth death. The law given to Moses required human effort and action, but when grace and truth appeared in the form of Christ, the responsibility was taken off human flesh and put upon Him. The old nature, though it recognizes this truth, will not submit to the rule of God and will not be converted because it cannot attain unto this higher law.

The old nature may utter these words but the spiritual heart is closed to the application of them. Thus the tortured soul wanders about in a state of wretchedness, forfeiting the mercy and frustrating the grace of God. It realizes that it is condemned, guilty of death and in need of redemption, but if it does not yield itself to God and become converted, it will go about to establish its own form of righteousness and have religious experiences, emotional highs, and a form of godliness but no power.

There will be no relationship with God through His Son, Jesus Christ. The praise will be noise, the prayers will be vain and without fervor, and though works will be done, the spirit behind them will not be of God. Sad to say, it will yet fool many a soul into believing that this is of God.

Does this wretched soul know the truth? Yes! Pride and arrogance, haughtiness and the love of pleasure (more than the love of God) have become its bedfellow. When confronted with truth, it turns away fearing that it may cost too much to rebuild what is truly castles in the air–a house that is built upon the sand and subject to fall at any given time. Herein lies the wonder of Paul's conversion.

This elite man of prestige and prodigious grandeur was on his way up the ladder of success. He had everything to gain and nothing to lose...so he thought. When he met Jesus on the road to Damascus (Acts 9), he was yet *"...breathing out threatening and slaughter against the disciples of the Lord."* He was a man of authority and could get his way because he knew and followed the law without error. He was a devout Jew, instructed according to the strict manner of the law; an illustrious Pharisee who was trained at the feet of the great rabbi, Gamaliel. Paul was Roman born, a Hebrew of Hebrews who had a radical passion and relentless endeavor to further his cause and he yet stands as the most able exponent and the most influential apostle of all time.

He was gifted with many natural qualities, was of high intellectual understanding, and fluent in Roman and Greek cultures; he was able to approach men of all classes. He appeared on the biblical scene already in a prominent position at the stoning of Stephen.

Being a man of impeccable understanding, he knew why the Pharisees were opposed to the ministry of Jesus. He had been given a thorough education of the Jewish law so he could not deny the works done by the Man who claimed to be the Messiah but to question the premise of his beliefs would jeopardize everything. His whole life was centered on Judaism. It was all he knew and hadn't he been taught by the most prestigious men in the field? Surely they knew the truth.

Imagine the confusion, the turmoil, and utter shock of being summoned...by the Lord. A humbled Saul realized that he did not know God but he feared Him. And according to Proverbs 1:5, *"the fear of the Lord is the beginning of knowledge."* He didn't see Jesus perform any miracles nor hear Him teach in parables, but when he heard His voice, he succumbed in child-like faith and immediately yielded to God's will.

At a time when he could have risen to the heights of popularity and success in the world, he counted the cost and left all to embrace the good news about Jesus Christ. He counted all that he had acquired prior to his conversion as dung and boldly declared that *"there is therefore now no condemnation to them, which are in Christ Jesus, who walk not after the flesh, but after the Spirit"* (Romans 8:1). He withstood his former companions without humiliation, fear, or intimidation stating that he was not ashamed of the Gospel of Christ. His beloved law became a stumbling block so he forsook even that and gave up all to follow Christ.

This is why Paul states in II Corinthians 5:16, *"...know we no man after the flesh."* He goes on to state that *"if any man be in Christ, he is a new creature: old things are passed away; behold, all things are become new and all things are of God."*

The old nature, the flesh, will be bound to sin if it does not embrace this truth. But hope remains undaunted in God, for if the unregenerate mind turns to God and becomes the servant of righteousness and obey from the heart (mind) that form of doctrine it can be delivered and freed from sin.

CHAPTER FIVE

HAVE I BEEN DECEIVED?

AT THIS POINT, YOU MAY FEEL weighted down with grief, sorrow, and shame. But take heart, God has brought you to this very point to make an informed decision. In fact, if you are feeling any of these things, it is good, for the Lord will not despise a broken and contrite heart (Psalm 51:17). He does not want His children to continue in error and states that if we continue in His Word, *"...ye shall know the truth, and the truth shall make you free"* (John 8:32).

Deception occurs when one has been misled to believe what is not true. The Bible affirms in Second Thessalonians that this is a sign that the day of Christ is at hand and God shall send a strong delusion that those who have rejected Him and rebelled against His Word might believe a lie.

But only those who have not received the love of truth will be caught in this deception. The passage in John 3:16 stating that God so loved the world and gave His only Son is probably the most common

Scripture known by all–sinner and saint alike. But when a gift is given, it can be accepted without being received.

Many years ago, a gift was given to me. I accepted the present from the giver, however not willingly. So the gift remained at my house, still wrapped in its original package for a long time. I had received the gift but until I unwrapped it, handled it and made use of it, I had not accepted it.

The complexity is the simplicity of that train of thought. When things contrary to the Spirit of truth are presented, they do not have to be accepted. We must admit that we have been deceived because we embraced a lie rather than the truth. Regardless of how it was presented, we attempted to go forth in life while still in the womb of the Spirit and allowed ourselves to be rushed through the process of repentance. We must honestly admit, we knew something was amiss and let the passing thought of "what am I lacking" keep running through our mind without stopping to reason with God.

When Moses saw the burning bush (Exodus 3), he turned aside (considered). Why was the bush burning with fire but not consumed? Scripture states that when the Lord saw that Moses turned aside to see this great sight, then He called unto him and spoke. Moses' response was simply, *"Here am I."*

We must take some responsibility for our current condition because God has appeared to us in ways that should have caught our attention.

We took note of some of these things, but did not "turn aside" to see why. Because we did not avail ourselves to Him, God did not speak.

Perhaps you did turn aside and see, and God spoke, but what was your response? Moses' response allowed a conversation to develop between him and God. At first he hid his face, being afraid, but then he reverenced the Lord and communed with Him. In the midst of their discourse, God got angry with Moses because he kept making excuses that went against His will. *"But His anger endureth but a moment"* (Psalm 30:5) and they kept talking until Moses finally placed himself in the hands of God.

Moses didn't readily accept all that was spoken to him and tried to get out of doing what was required of him, but he received the words of God and eventually acted in obedience. He looked honestly at himself, admitted his weaknesses and humbled himself before God.

All too often, we are deceived because we have believed a lie rather than the truth. We would fault the one who lied to us, but in all fairness, had we guarded our heart and mind with all diligence we would not have received that package when it was delivered. Neither the preacher, teacher, nor prophet lied to me. I lied to myself. The Lord does want to pour out and bless His children, but we must be in a position to receive. Have I been seeking the blessings or the Blesser?

Moses could have returned to Midian after seeing the burning bush and continued to be a herdsman; he could often ponder the conversation held with God and wonder, "Lord, when will you make me a great leader?" Well, until he positioned himself and went to Egypt, it was not going to happen.

For too long we've received true revelations from God, gotten prophetic words spoken over us and into our lives and then returned to the same old routine. Now if that's the directive given by God, so be it. But when He says, *"go, and sin no more"* (John 8:11), He means just that. Too often we begin to pursue the blessing rather than seeking His kingdom and His righteousness (Matthew 6:33).

After Jesus was crucified, He had shown Himself to the disciples and yet, the day came (before His ascension) that Peter, the one who boldly declared that Jesus was the Christ, the Son of God, and then later denied Him, stated, *"I go a fishing"* (John 21:3). He, along with six of the other disciples, went back to what they had been called from. If they had continued fishing at the sea of Tiberias rather than tarrying in Jerusalem, they would not have been in position for the outpouring of the Holy Spirit.

There have been times, when in the presence of God, He chastised me and I stood humbly before Him. But in so doing, saints around me would whisper, "God's releasing a mighty anointing upon you." My hands were uplifted in surrender–but I heard God's voice of correction within my spirit. Yes, I liked what the saints were saying more than the reproof I was getting from God, but truth prevailed.

I had to turn a deaf ear to what they were saying and heed what the Lord was telling me. I knew the condition I was in and could have easily gone along with what others assumed was occurring, but I would have allowed myself to be deceived.

After Peter declared that Jesus was the Christ (Matthew 16), the next thing Peter uttered was an offence to the Messiah. The Lord began to tell the disciples about what He must suffer and prophesied about His own death. But Peter rebuked the Lord and said, *"be it far from Thee, Lord: this shall not be unto you."*

The Lord, however, saw the spirit behind the words and replied to Peter, *"get thee behind me satan: thou art an offence unto me: for thou savourest not the things that be of God, but those that be of men"* (vs. 23). Now the Lord could have taken comfort in what Peter was saying, but He knew truth and did not receive or accept the lie spoken by satan through Peter. Nor did He rebuke Peter but rather the spirit of satan that was at work.

All too often, when deception occurs it is because we wrestled with flesh and blood and did not separate the spirit from the speaker. Satan knows the Word of God and will twist and misconstrue the very things spoken by Him. He'll speak half-truths, and in all subtlety will have us believe a lie rather than the truth. For example, the familiar passage in Romans 8:28 states, *"For we know that all things work together for the good of them that love God, to them who are the called according to* **His** *purpose."*

Emphasis is put upon the word "His" purpose. If I don't love God and am working to achieve my own ambitions without knowing the will of God for my life, then all things are not working together for the good. Far too many souls who lack relationship with God through His Son are attempting to apply the promises of God to their lives, and though the principle may work, God is under no obligation to fulfill the desires of this person's heart.

Not so long ago, it seems the whole country was ablaze with the *Prayer of Jabez*. Books were written and sinner and saint alike formed the habit of uttering the prayer daily, expecting God to grant their requests. Many did not take time to read the entire passage but simply "jumped on the band wagon" and began quoting this prayer. And nothing, by any means, is wrong with the prayer.

But the verse above the prayer declares, *"and Jabez was more honorable than his brethren...."* (I Chronicles 4:9). He was a man of integrity and made this petition to God in accordance to His purpose. The end of verse ten states that *"God granted him that which he requested."* How many who prayed this prayer, when its awareness was heightened, have this testimony?

Furthermore, in II Corinthians 1:20, the Bible declares that all the promises of God in Him are *"yea, and in Him, Amen, unto the glory of God by us."* Many have adopted this scriptural text as words to live by and bless God, but unless you are "in Christ" these promises are not at work in your life.

So the enemy works deceptive measures to keep us from being *"in Christ."* He makes the distinction so fine that it can be difficult to detect or analyze truth from error. So first, it behooves us to ensure that before we embrace the promises of God, we know with all assuredness that we are indeed in Christ. Now the Bible explicitly states what the works of the flesh are and states that *"they, which do such things, shall not inherit the kingdom of God"* (Romans 1:18-32; I Corinthians 3:3; Galatians 5:19-21; Colossians 3:5).

So if these works are being manifested in our lives, yet we claim we are full of the Spirit of God, we lie and do not speak the truth. And if one lives in expectancy of the promises of God while practicing the works of the flesh in their mortal body, they are deceiving themselves.

Another form of deception is the wistful belief that one can *"call those things that be not as though they were"* (Romans 4:17). Again, the enemy has wrought deception and many have embraced a half-truth. This statement is only a portion of an entire verse and speaks of faith. Abraham believed God, thus what God had spoken to him was embraced as truth. All too often, we attempt to apply this Scripture to things we desire, things we want to occur in our lives but have never been spoken by God.

Because Abraham had a relationship with God and had made a covenant with Him (Genesis 15:17-18), the things that God spoke into his life could be counted as truth. The fulfillment was in accordance to God's timing and was to be brought about God's way, Abraham simply believed. This belief was proven by his acts of obedience.

So one must ask, is my belief in the promises of God dictating my actions? Am I resting in the promises of God and waiting in quiet expectation for the fulfillment as God sees fit to unfold His purpose in my life and in the way He so chooses?

There are false prophets and preachers who were not sent by God going forth in the ministry, but as Christ rebuked Satan when he spoke through Peter, to adhere to things that are not of God is to cling to things that are of Satan. But he would have us to believe that we have many options, many choices to make, but know the truth as given in Romans 6:16: *"Know ye not, that to whom ye yield yourselves servants to obey, his servants ye are to whom ye obey; whether of sin unto death, or of obedience unto righteousness."*

Be it also known unto you that God will use His chosen vessels to speak to the idols in your heart. Ezekiel, a choice prophet of the Lord was commanded to speak to the elders of Israel things that were pleasing to them, while they were in rebellion against God (Ezekiel 14). They were seeking the blessings of God while breaking the covenant between them.

Judge within yourselves: am I getting everything I desire because I am blessed by God while living in accordance to His will for my life?

Or am I receiving things according to the multitude of idols in my heart? We can only examine ourselves and open our heart to God for He alone knoweth and trieth the heart of man.

When Satan stood before the Lord desiring to have his way with Job, he revealed a profound truth that should encourage all saints. God has a hedge about His children and about all their substance: their children, jobs, home, etc (Job 1:6-10). The enemy cannot penetrate that hedge without the permission of God but Solomon states in Ecclesiastes 10:8, *"...whoso breaketh an hedge, a serpent shall bite him."*

That serpent is Satan. His venom is poisonous and can only be cleansed by the blood of Jesus. There are many snake-bitten souls wandering through life in a daze. They've broken the hedge of protection and as the venom gains strength, their [spiritual] senses become dulled and feeling the sickness within and without, their very life begins to seep out.

They simply exist, living well beneath the means of what God ordained for them. Their life is not abundant, there is no joy that's unspeakable or full of glory, and the sweet fellowship with the Lord seems unobtainable. But there is yet hope. Even if you are the only one who knows about the darkened room within your heart, it is not hid from God. Return to that room, allow the light of His love to flood into the darkness, confess your faults to the Father and be ye converted for the saving of your soul.

CHAPTER SIX

CONVINCED OF MY CONVERSION

CONVERSION, FROM THE HEBREW WORD, *SHUV,* has it's basic meaning as movement back to the point of departure, that is, Genesis 3:19 where punishment is meted out to Adam: *"In the sweat of thy face shalt thou eat bread, till thou return unto the ground; for out of it wast thou taken: for dust thou art, and unto dust shalt thou return."*

Neither Adam nor Eve were cursed by God. Satan, disguised as a serpent, was cursed. The ground also was cursed for the serpent goes upon it on his belly and eats the dust (man). To be cursed is to have an appeal for evil or injury to befall someone or something; it is a profane oath. So to believe that God cursed man is not true; man was judged, found guilty and punished for his rebellion against God.

Peter asserts in his second epistle that *"the Lord is not willing that any should perish, but that all should come to repentance"* (3:9). When the woman was taken in adultery, caught in the very act, after her accusers were gone away, Jesus says, *"...neither do I condemn you, go and sin no more"* (John 8:11). If Christ would not denounce a woman caught in the very act of adultery, neither will He forsake or curse His own.

Man is a spirit being, with a soul, encased in a body. The body is composed of the dust of the earth and this earthen vessel will return from the dust from whence it came.

The Greek word for conversion is *epistrophe*, which is to turn away from; a turning oneself around. At the point of salvation, a new nature is given to the believer–a renewed spirit. And what is given within must be worked without.

As the fetus upon birth, no longer is dependent upon the umbilical cord for nourishment and removal of bodily wastes through the mother, no longer can the regenerated soul idly expect to survive. The renewed spirit must grow and develop in the knowledge of Christ. As the renewed soul seeks to know God and develops a bond of fellowship with Him through His Spirit, the manifestation of what is believed is displayed through their actions.

One turns away from the former way of doing things, and seeks to know the will and the way of God for any given situation. Peter states it this way: *"As obedient children, not fashioning yourselves according to the former lusts in your ignorance"* (I Peter 1:14). The carnal mind has been denounced and the renewed mind, the mind of Christ, is the perspective that things are seen.

It's more than not going where one used to go and not doing the things one used to do. It profits very little if in the heart one longs and desires for the "old" way but has no means of satisfying the flesh. If that desire is not rooted out, a spiritual high that is currently being experienced is the only constraint. Jude gives way to the One Who is able to keep us from falling, so in turning away from the carnal mind, one turns to the One Who can keep them.

I don't try to keep myself no more than I can attempt to convert my own soul. I submit my will to God that desires to be kept by Him so that even when the old nature attempts to exert itself, I look to God to keep me from falling and to give me power to overcome that desire.

Conversion is a continual part of the believers' process in pressing toward the mark for the prize of the high calling of God in Jesus Christ (Philippians 4:14). Just as Christ said he would, Peter denied that he knew Him. But with true repentance, Peter turned himself around and was restored. Judas, on the other hand, after betraying Christ, did not turn himself around and losing all hope, committed suicide.

We are a people with a hope, and unlike Judas, we will not repent unto man, but to a holy God against Whom only we have sinned. To be convinced of your conversion, allow Him to search your innermost being and be completely honest with His diagnosis. Do not deny what you know to be true. A simple, "Yes, Lord," will allow the chaotic chambers within your heart to be set in order.

If you have found the only thing you are consistent with is inconsistency, perhaps conversion has not occurred. If you feel the need to pray more, fast more, read more of the Word, but lack the spiritual power to carry out these deeds, perhaps conversion has not occurred. If you seek spiritual highs, emotional charges, and religious experiences rather than an intimate relationship with a holy God, then perhaps conversion has not occurred.

Conversion occurs within the heart and is manifested when one seeks to know the will of God and is willing to wait on the Spirit to teach them the ways of God. We cannot reach a holy God, who is a Spirit, by simply doing good deeds and natural acts when the motivation comes from our own initiative. The converted soul is one that accepts the ongoing process of learning to please God by being willing and obedient to whatever the Spirit leads them to do. Paul states in Romans 8:14, *"for as many as are led by the Spirit of God, they are the sons of God."*

Acts 8:9-24 records the incident of one Simon, the sorcerer; he believed and was baptized along with many other Samaritans, however, he was not converted. Consider Peter's response to him when he sought to purchase the gift of the Holy Ghost with money, *"...thou hast neither part nor lot in this matter for thy heart is not right in the sight of God. Repent therefore of this thy wickedness, and pray God, if perhaps the thought of thine heart may be forgiven thee."*

Because his heart was not right, he sought to obtain the things of God through natural means. After his baptism, rather than seeking to know the God Who had saved him, he was in awe of the miracles and wonders being done by the disciples. He sought the blessings rather than the Blesser and thought the disciples could give him something that only comes from God.

The gift is the Holy Ghost. He is the power behind the works of wonder and miracles. Believers who have this gift can do all things because it's not them, but the Spirit at work within them. Sadly, we must admit, many Simons are on the battlefield seeking to do the works themselves rather than allowing the Spirit to be at work within them.

Peter simply told Simon to repent.

A heart of repentance is necessary for the process of conversion to remain at work in the life of the believer. When Simon was corrected by Peter and told to repent, his response to the apostle was, *"...pray ye to the Lord for me...."* His repentance is not recorded but we know that no matter how fervently Peter may have prayed for him, if he did not repent, the prayers were of no avail. And though he believed and was baptized, if not repentant of his heart condition, he was never converted.

So let us consider why repentance is such a vital component of conversion. Peter told Simon that his heart was not right in the sight of God. Now Simon believed, was baptized, and continued with Philip who was a man of honest report and full of the Holy Ghost and wisdom (Acts 6:3, 5). But Simon's "hook-up" with Philip did not cause a change within his heart nor validate his conversion.

It is recorded in Jeremiah 17:9 that the heart is deceitful above all things, and desperately wicked but goes on stating that the Lord searches the heart and gives every man according to his ways and according to the fruit of his doings. Only God can create a clean heart within the believer and renew the right Spirit within (Psalm 51).

Many are trying to obey God by doing what they think He wants in a way they think is appropriate rather than staying in fellowship with the Spirit of God, allowing Him to give instruction and direction. He knows the heart of God and seeks to impart God's will into our everyday life. God is too meticulous in His dealings with us for us to be second-guessing or having a "Plan B" to fall back on. Too much human effort or intervention by man is not being Spirit-led. How often He speaks and we turn a deaf ear to what He has spoken or worse yet, we hear but set off to comply through our own efforts and in our own way.

Conversion is necessary for one to change from the old nature to the new, for in this process, the flesh, which is enmity to God, is changed into a new creature. This regenerated spirit develops a hunger for the things of God and seeks fellowship with Him.

It desires to have a bond, to be infused by the Spirit of God, to be acceptable to a holy God. Every believer must be persuaded in his own mind of his conversion. The old nature will not attain to the things of God but when one sees the need for a Savior and submits his will to God, conversion will occur—and when thou art converted, strengthen thy brethren.

Traces of Greatness

What is in me
that will speak
encouragement to hearts
known and unknown

That causes spirits
to rise, to swell
assured of the
victory

It's not always there
with such intensity.
Sometimes it's only
trickles, strands or
fleeting moments;

But it's never
completely gone
always hovering
in my spirit,
my mind, my heart

We have this treasure
in earthen vessels that
the excellency of the
power is in God
Not us...

–Anna Marie Davis

The Plan of Salvation

Conversion cannot occur if you have never accepted Jesus Christ as your personal Savior. Allow Him to become Lord of your life and begin to enjoy the benefits of life within the kingdom of God. Here's how:

1. Accept the fact that you are a sinner, and that you have broken God's law. The Bible says in Ecclesiastes 7:20: *"For there is not a just man upon earth that doeth good, and sinneth not."* Romans 3:23: *"For all have sinned and come short of the glory of God."*

2. Accept the fact that there is a penalty for sin. The Bible states in Romans 6:23: *"For the wages of sin is death..."*

3. Accept the fact that you are on the road to hell. Jesus Christ said in Matthew 10:28: *"And fear not them which kill the body, but are not able to kill the soul: but rather fear him which is able to destroy both soul and body in hell."*

The Bible says in Revelation 21:8: *"But the fearful, and unbelieving, and the abominable, and murderers, and whoremongers and sorcerers, and idolaters, and all liars, shall have their part in the lake which burneth with fire and brimstone: which is the second death."*

4. **Accept the fact that you cannot do anything to save yourself!** The Bible states in Ephesians 2: 8, 9: *"For by grace are ye saved through faith: and that not of yourselves: it is a gift of God. Not of works, lest any man should boast."*

5. **Accept the fact that God loves you more than you love yourself, and that He wants to save you from hell.** *"For God so loved the world, that He gave His only begotten Son, that whosoever believeth in Him should not perish, but have everlasting life"* (John 3:16).

6. With these facts in mind, please repent of your sins, believe on the Lord Jesus Christ and pray and ask Him to come into your heart and save you this very moment.

The Bible states in the book of Romans 10:9, 13: *"That if thou shalt confess with thy mouth the Lord Jesus, and shalt believe in thine heart that God hath raised Him from the dead, thou shalt be saved." "For whosoever shall call upon the name of the Lord shall be saved."*

7. If you are willing to trust Christ as your Saviour and receive the power of the Holy Ghost in your life, please pray with me the following prayer:

Heavenly Father, I realize that I am a sinner and that I have sinned against you. For Jesus Christ's sake, please forgive me of all of my sins. I now believe with all of my heart that Jesus Christ died, was buried, and rose again for me. Lord Jesus, please come into my heart, save my soul, change my life, and fill me with your Holy Ghost today and forever. Amen.

Contact Information:
Touch of Grace
(512) 248-1740
b.roscoe@earthlink.net

Made in the USA
Charleston, SC
22 February 2010